Behind My Eyes

Also by Li-Young Lee

The Undressing

Book of My Nights

The City in Which I Love You

Rose

The Winged Seed: A Remembrance

Behind My Eyes

Li-Young Lee

W · W · Norton & Company

New York   London

For information about permission to reproduce selections
from this book, write to Permissions,
W. W. Norton & Company, Inc.,
500 Fifth Avenue, New York, NY 10110

For information about special discounts for bulk purchases, please contact
W. W. Norton Special Sales at specialsales@wwnorton.com or 800-233-4830

Manufacturing by Courier Westford
Book design by Margaret M. Wagner
Production manager: Julia Druskin

Library of Congress Cataloging-in-Publication Data

Lee, Li-Young, 1957–
Behind my eyes / Li-Young Lee. — 1st ed.
p. cm.
Poems.
ISBN 978-0-393-06542-8 (hardcover)
ISBN 978-0-393-33481-4 (softcover)
I. Title.
PS3562.E35438B45 2008
811'.54—dc22   2007035465

W. W. Norton & Company, Inc.
500 Fifth Avenue, New York, N.Y. 10110
www.wwnorton.com

W. W. Norton & Company Ltd.
15 Carlisle Street, London W1D 3BS

4 5 6 7 8 9 0

For my mother

Contents

I

In His Own Shadow *15*

Self-Help for Fellow Refugees *16*

Mother Deluxe *19*

Become Becoming *21*

Have You Prayed *23*

A Hymn to Childhood *25*

Immigrant Blues *28*

Sweet Peace in Time *30*

Seven Happy Endings *33*

Lake Effect *36*

Trading for Heaven *41*

II

My Favorite Kingdom *45*

Evening Hieroglyph *47*

First World *48*

The Mother's Apple *50*

The Father's Apple *51*

The Apple Elopes *52*

My Clothes Lie Folded for the Journey *54*

To Life *56*

Seven Marys *57*

Descended from Dreamers *60*

Parable of the Jar   62

Little Ache   63

Cuckoo Flower on the Witness Stand   64

After the Pyre   66

The Sea with Fish   68

Changing Places in the Fire   69

III

God Seeks a Destiny   75

Secret Life   77

The Lives of a Voice   79

The Shortcut Home   88

Standard Checklist for Amateur Mystics   89

Bring Home Her Name   90

A Winter Day   91

Virtues of the Boring Husband   92

To Hold   98

Living with Her   99

Dying Stupid   102

Station   104

Acknowledgments   107

Behind My Eyes

In His Own Shadow

He is seated in the first darkness
of his body sitting in the lighter dark
of the room,

the greater light of day behind him,
beyond the windows, where
Time is the country.

His body throws two shadows:
One onto the table
and the piece of paper before him,
and one onto his mind.

One makes it difficult for him to see
the words he's written and crossed out
on the paper. The other
keeps him from recognizing
another master than Death. He squints.
He reads: *Does the first light hide
inside the first dark?*

He reads: *While all bodies share
the same fate, all voices do not.*

Self-Help for Fellow Refugees

If your name suggests a country where bells
might have been used for entertainment

or to announce the entrances and exits of the seasons
or the birthdays of gods and demons,

it's probably best to dress in plain clothes
when you arrive in the United States,
and try not to talk too loud.

If you happen to have watched armed men
beat and drag your father
out the front door of your house
and into the back of an idling truck

before your mother jerked you from the threshold
and buried your face in her skirt folds,
try not to judge your mother too harshly.

Don't ask her what she thought she was doing
turning a child's eyes
away from history
and toward that place all human aching starts.

And if you meet someone
in your adopted country,
and think you see in the other's face
an open sky, some promise of a new beginning,
it probably means you're standing too far.

Or if you think you read in the other, as in a book
whose first and last pages are missing,
the story of your own birthplace,
a country twice erased,
once by fire, once by forgetfulness,
it probably means you're standing too close.

In any case, try not to let another carry
the burden of your own nostalgia or hope.

And if you're one of those
whose left side of the face doesn't match
the right, it might be a clue

looking the other way was a habit
your predecessors found useful for survival.
Don't lament not being beautiful.

Get used to seeing while not seeing.
Get busy remembering while forgetting.
Dying to live while not wanting to go on.

Very likely, your ancestors decorated
their bells of every shape and size
with elaborate calendars
and diagrams of distant star systems,
but with no maps for scattered descendants.

＊　＊

And I bet you can't say what language
your father spoke when he shouted to your mother
from the back of the truck, "Let the boy see!"

Maybe it wasn't the language you used at home.
Maybe it was a forbidden language.
Or maybe there was too much screaming
and weeping and the noise of guns in the streets.

It doesn't matter. What matters is this:
The kingdom of heaven is good.
But heaven on earth is better.

Thinking is good.
But living is better.

Alone in your favorite chair
with a book you enjoy
is fine. But spooning
is even better.

Mother Deluxe

"We can't stay where we are,
and we don't know where else to go,"

is the first card my mother deals. We're playing
her deluxe edition of "Memories
from the 20th Century."

"Dead Baby," "Mystery Bundles," "Cleansing by Sacrifice."

Seven cards apiece and the object is to not die.

"Exodus," "Eyes Snatched Away,"
"Superstition at the Side of the Road."

All cards are good or bad depending on how you play them.
"Defeated by Wings," "Eating Forbidden Blood."

No card possesses inherent value.
"Among the Lepers," "Burial by the Solo River,"
"The Extracted Oil."

Every player begins in bondage.
Every player eventually dies. Everybody plays
whether they know or don't know they're playing.

Maybe this isn't a game.
Maybe it's the World Evening News.

    . .

Maybe this time I'll rescue my mother.
I can't tell if I thought that or if she said it.

Maybe this isn't the news.
Maybe this is a dream God is having
and somebody should wake Him.

Good boat, first boat, old boat, Mother,
my first night with you lasted nine months.
Our second night together is the rest of my life.

Become Becoming

Wait for evening.
Then you'll be alone.

Wait for the playground to empty.
Then call out those companions from childhood:

The one who closed his eyes
and pretended to be invisible.
The one to whom you told every secret.
The one who made a world of any hiding place.

And don't forget the one who listened in silence
while you wondered out loud:

Is the universe an empty mirror? A flowering tree?
Is the universe the sleep of a woman?

Wait for the sky's last blue
(the color of your homesickness).
Then you'll know the answer.

Wait for the air's first gold (that color of *Amen*).
Then you'll spy the wind's barefoot steps.

Then you'll recall that story beginning
with a child who strays in the woods.

. .

The search for him goes on in the growing
shadow of the clock.

And the face behind the clock's face
is not his father's face.

And the hands behind the clock's hands
are not his mother's hands.

All of Time began when you first answered
to the names your mother and father gave you.

Soon, those names will travel with the leaves.
Then, you can trade places with the wind.

Then you'll remember your life
as a book of candles,
each page read by the light of its own burning.

Have You Prayed

When the wind
turns and asks, in my father's voice,
Have you prayed?

I know three things. One:
I'm never finished answering to the dead.

Two: A man is four winds and three fires.
And the four winds are his father's voice,
his mother's voice . . .

Or maybe he's seven winds and ten fires.
And the fires are seeing, hearing, touching,
dreaming, thinking . . .
Or is he the breath of God?

When the wind turns traveler
and asks, in my father's voice, *Have you prayed?*
I remember three things.
One: A father's love

is milk and sugar,
two-thirds worry, two-thirds grief, and what's left over

is trimmed and leavened to make the bread
the dead and the living share.

. .

And patience? That's to endure
the terrible leavening and kneading.

And wisdom? That's my father's face in sleep.

When the wind
asks, *Have you prayed?*
I know it's only me

reminding myself
a flower is one station between
earth's wish and earth's rapture, and blood

was fire, salt, and breath long before
it quickened any wand or branch, any limb
that woke speaking. It's just me

in the gowns of the wind,
or my father through me, asking,
Have you found your refuge yet?
asking, *Are you happy?*

Strange. A troubled father. A happy son.
The wind with a voice. And me talking to no one.

A Hymn to Childhood

Childhood? Which childhood?
The one that didn't last?
The one in which you learned to be afraid
of the boarded-up well in the backyard
and the ladder to the attic?

The one presided over by armed men
in ill-fitting uniforms
strolling the streets and alleys,
while loudspeakers declared a new era,
and the house around you grew bigger,
the rooms farther apart, with more and more
people missing?

The photographs whispered to each other
from their frames in the hallway.
The cooking pots said your name
each time you walked past the kitchen.

And you pretended to be dead with your sister
in games of rescue and abandonment.
You learned to lie still so long
the world seemed a play you viewed from the muffled
safety of a wing. Look! In
run the servants screaming, the soldiers shouting,
turning over the furniture,
smashing your mother's china.

. .

Don't fall asleep.
Each act opens with your mother
reading a letter that makes her weep.
Each act closes with your father fallen
into the hands of Pharaoh.

Which childhood? The one that never ends? O you,
still a child, and slow to grow.
Still talking to God and thinking the snow
falling is the sound of God listening,
and winter is the high-ceilinged house
where God measures with one eye
an ocean wave in octaves and minutes,
and counts on many fingers
all the ways a child learns to say *Me*.

Which childhood?
The one from which you'll never escape? You,
so slow to know
what you know and don't know.
Still thinking you hear low song
in the wind in the eaves,
story in your breathing,
grief in the heard dove at evening,
and plentitude in the unseen bird
tolling at morning. Still slow to tell

memory from imagination, heaven
from here and now,
hell from here and now,
death from childhood, and both of them
from dreaming.

Immigrant Blues

People have been trying to kill me since I was born,
a man tells his son, trying to explain
the wisdom of learning a second tongue.

It's an old story from the previous century
about my father and me.

The same old story from yesterday morning
about me and my son.

It's called "Survival Strategies
and the Melancholy of Racial Assimilation."

It's called "Psychological Paradigms of Displaced Persons,"

called "The Child Who'd Rather Play than Study."

Practice until you feel
the language inside you, says the man.

But what does he know about inside and outside,
my father who was spared nothing
in spite of the languages he used?

And me, confused about the flesh and the soul,
who asked once into a telephone,
Am I inside you?

. .

You're always inside me, a woman answered,
at peace with the body's finitude,
at peace with the soul's disregard
of space and time.

Am I inside you? I asked once
lying between her legs, confused
about the body and the heart.

If you don't believe you're inside me, you're not,
she answered, at peace with the body's greed,
at peace with the heart's bewilderment.

It's an ancient story from yesterday evening

called "Patterns of Love in Peoples of Diaspora,"

called "Loss of the Homeplace
and the Defilement of the Beloved,"

called "I Want to Sing but I Don't Know Any Songs."

Sweet Peace in Time

I said, "What if by *story* you mean *the shortcut home,*
but I mean *voices in a room by the sea*
while days go by?"

She said, "Open, The Word is a child of eternity.
Closed, The Word is a child of Time."

I said, "And what if by *dream* you mean *to comb*
the knots out of your hair,

to prune the orchard
and correct the fruit,

but I mean *to travel*
by rain crossing the sea, or apple blossoms
traversing a stone threshold
with a word carved into it: Abyss?"

She said, "Home, speech is the living purchase
of our nights and days.

A traveler, it is a voice in its own lifetime.

A river, it is Time sifted, Time manifest,
laughter that sires the rocks and trees,
that fetches in its ancient skirts
the fateful fruits and seeds."

    . .

I said, "And what if when I say, *Song*,
you hear, *A wing*

executing boundary by sounding
the range of its hunting,

but I mean *Time and the World*
measured by a voice's passage?"

She said, "Empty, The Word is a wind in the trees.

Full, it is the voice of a woman
reading out loud from a book of names."

I said, "To speak is to err.
Words name nothing.
There are no words."

She said, "Lure, slaughter, feast, blood
in the throat, words turn, changing."

I said, "We should give up
trying to speak or to be understood.
It's too late in the world for dialogue.

. .

Death creates a blind spot.
Man is a secret, blind to himself.
And woman . . . Woman is . . ."

She said, "Our meeting here manifests
a primordial threshold.

A first and last place, speech
is no place at all, a shelter, ark, and cradle;

salt but not salt, bread but not bread,
a house but no house."

I said, "The garden was ruined long before
we came to make a world of it."

Seven Happy Endings

Love, after talking all night,
where are we? Where did we begin?

I needed to name this, needed to know
what we meant when we said *we*,
when we said *us*, when we said *this*.

I wanted to call it something:
Shadows on the garden wall.
A man rowing alone out to sea.
Seven happy endings.

And you? You were happy
with two rooms, and a door to divide them.
And daylight on either side of the door.
Borrowed music from an upstairs room.
And bells from down the street
to urge our salty hearts.

But I woke up one night
and realized I was falling.
I turned on the lamp and the lamp was falling.
And the hand that turned on the lamp was falling.
And the light was falling, and everything the light touched
falling. And you were falling
asleep beside me.
And that was the first happy ending.

. .

And the last one?
It went something like this:

A child sat down, opened a book,
and began to read. And what he read out loud
came to pass. And what he kept to himself
stayed on the other side of the mountains.

But I promised seven happy endings.
I who know nothing about endings.
I who am always at the beginning of everything.
Even as our being together
always feels like beginning.
Not just the beginning of our knowing each other,
but the beginning of reality itself.

See how you and I
make this room so quiet with our presence.

With every word we say
the room grows quieter.

With every word we keep ourselves
from speaking, even quieter.

And now I don't know where we are.
Still needing to call it something:

The fountain's water
ringing the lip of the rock.

A clock the bees unearth,
gathering the overspilled minutes.

Lake Effect

She said, "The lake is like an open book,
day like the steady gaze of a reader."

I said, "The day is a book we open between us,
the lake a sentence we read together
over and over, our voices
ghost, bread, and horizon."

She said, "A spoken song in several voices
moving in and out of many rooms."

I said, "The mind like a lake,
and your voice a figure of the foam."

She said, "The book a voice, its pages
burning in rooms birds foretell every evening."

I said, "The lake keeps changing its mind,
undecided between
the word for the end of August
and the color just before grapes ripen."

She said, "The book summons the reader
to read the laws of water, wind, fire, dust,
and the destiny of voices."

I said, "Voices in a room by the lake,
the lake itself an older voice, unutterable
law and companion

to a brother and sister telling
each other the missing parts
of each other's stories."

She said, "The lake is a book. Open the book
and the book says:

The world is full of people, but seldom
is a person to be found.

The world is full of light, yet who
has seen such a thing?

The world is all dark, yet a hand finds its way
to other hands, a mouth its way to another mouth."

I said, "The lake keeps changing its mind,
a book turning,

now the shadows of clouds on the pages,
now the shadows of pages on the waves."

She said, "Shadows of birds
and leaves blown in a wind
have fallen on the book,

birds and clouds and leaves in silent tumult
among the pages.

. .

Day is a gate, an illegible stone,
a garden, a woman with a book open in her lap.

And the book says: *Silver,*
the women sing of their bodies and the men.

Darker, the men sing of their ancestors and the women.

Darkest is the children's ambition
to sing every circle wider.

Dying, each sings at the edge of what he knows.

Inside us is the unknown, that chasm
singing makes visible by overleaping."

I said, "The lake is an unblinking glare,
a single page turning in day's fire."

She said, "The page is shadowed by a reader's face."

I said, "The book turns in the clear fire
of the reader's gaze.
The voices in the book arrive like waves."

She said, "The waves arrive like the unfolding
sum of our days speaking."

．　．

I said, "The pages are traveling,
the book is without horizon,

and over the foam-flecked body of fire,
hands keep changing places with wings.

Therefore, a voice was first, the world comes after,
and the book comes last.

Open the book and the book says:

*Ash and dew sing the founding notes
of world, book, time, and body.*

The page remains the place where we can hear them."

She said, "Voices lie toppled, confused
on the open pages. When the voices move,
we hear who is who.

A wind blows, the book is open
to a voice at evening
asking, *Are we many or one?*

*What do the past lives of the color blue have to do
with the fate of words and the future of wishing?*"

．　．

I said, "The lake's blue is the very memory of green.
The waves whiten as evening grows darker."

She said, "Time is a roasted egg, a sewing basket.
Time is the names of ships, a history of kite making.

Birds, turning in a flock, are a fleeting shape
of Time's deafening voice."

I said, "The shadows of birds on a page
almost tell a story."

She said, "My gaze clouds the page of your face."

I said, "Even in this boundless space,
if both of us turned our faces
toward each other at the same time

our mouths would be separated by an interval
a moth could not fly through without touching
both of what we said."

She said, "The lake, the first and last page of the day,
overwhelms every word written there."

I said, "So who was running down the steps
in front of the museum in the rain?
Who woke up sitting in the window of a moving train?"

Trading for Heaven

I saw you at the top of the stairs.
Now I live a secret life.

I saw you holding open the door.
Now I'm filling pages with

things I can't tell anyone.
Now I'm more alone than I've ever been.

I traded every beyond, every *someday*,
for heaven in my lifetime. Now I'm dying

of my life. Now I'm alive
inside my death.

Do you see the space between our bodies?
Barely a hand, hardly a breath,

it is the space mountains and rivers are made of.
It is the beginning of oceans, the space

between *either* and *or*, *both* and *neither*,
the happiness of forgetting

our names and the happiness of hearing them
for the first time. I heard you

singing yourself to sleep.
It was a song from both of our childhoods.

. .

And now I don't know if singing
is a form of helplessness,
Time's architecture revealed,

or some inborn motive all blood
and breath obey
to enact a savage wheel.

I found you at dawn
sitting by the open kitchen window.
You were sorting seeds in a plate.

And if you were praying out loud,
I'll never tell.

And if you were listening to the doves,
and if their various whoo-ing, and coo-ing,
and dying in time,
are your earliest questions blown back to you
through the ragged seasons,

and if you've lived your life
in answer to those questions,
I'll never tell.

Your destiny is safe with me.
Your childhood is safe with me.
What you decide to bury is safe with me.

My Favorite Kingdom

My favorite day is Sunday.

My favorite color is
my father's apple trees in the rain.

My favorite color
is my father's pear trees
in a cloud of bees.

My favorite day is Tuesday.

My favorite window
looks onto two oceans:

one a house
in various stages of ruin and beginning,

and one a book,
whose every word is outcome,
whose every page is lifelong sentence.

My favorite song is Time.

My favorite dream
is the one in which I stop
with my mother under branches
on the long way home from school.

· ·

My favorite room is in the branches
of the apple tree.

My favorite time of day
is when no one can find me.

My favorite door opens two ways:
receiving and receiving. My heart

swings between the ways, from thanksgiving
to thanksgiving, a thousand times a day,

while its naked feet graze
death's knobby head
a thousand times a day.

Evening Hieroglyph

Birds keep changing places in the empty tree
like decimals or numerals reconfiguring

some word which, spoken, might sound the key
that rights the tumblers in the iron lock
that keeps the gate dividing me from me.

Late January. The birds face all
one direction and flit
from branch to branch.

They raise no voice
against or for oncoming dark, no answer
to questions asked by one
whose entire being seems a question

posed to himself, one no longer new
on earth, unknowing, and yet,
still not the next thing.

First World

Sister, we died in childhood, remember?
Into birds we died, into their flying.

Toward all of sky we perished so completely
our mother cried, "Where are my little ones?"

Into her voice we died, that white singing
dispersed in day's greater sentence. And the days,

we disappeared into them and what they confided,
coming and going, but where?

Of noon we died, and of midnight, our longings
the bridges we built toward the future,

longings we wove in secret out of worry,
wonder, and expectancy.

And we died of the future,
of calling and mission only we could keep,

leaping into every favorite season;
sinking into roots, dreams, and books.

Nights beyond the house, we looked up and fell
into the known configurations of stars.

Nights, housed and in bed, we closed our eyes
and died into the unknown constellations:

the empty basket, the jeweled stair,
the table set for a guest.

Into our names we died, then past their precincts,
and would not be persuaded

the world lay kept in other, bigger hands.
Our secret? Where we stood, there stood all worlds.

We died, and we go on dying.
So where would I look for us except
in everything I see.

The Mother's Apple

I'm my mother's apple and that's that.
My sweetening draws death nearer, it can't be helped.
My bitterness about it is skin deep.
I'm told I'm a fourfold mystery
like the planet, but I think more.
I mean, there are tears inside me I'll never weep.
I'm heavy with unimaginable winters.
And though I'm told
apples come from apples, I believe
there must be a star somewhere among my ancestry,
and a bee, a map, a piano, and a shipwreck.
The blossoms give themselves to the wind.
Who will I be given to?
Rumor says, one day all of the iron keys
will spill out of the wind's pockets,
and each key will open a door to a mansion.
And one is named *Mind*,
and one is named *Abyss*,
and one is named *Life*,
and one is named *Work*,
and one is named *Love*.
Until then, I'll sit beneath this fragrant lintel,
the falling petals thunderous.

The Father's Apple

He says I won't always be an apple.
Descended from a book,
that is my chief end, he says.
But where do they keep all those petals?
I wonder. He says they're numbered.
He says their descent unearths
a consequent thirst
and several gaps in my history
as a falling body,
whose long-gone steps
led through Egypt and China.
Sweetness is a foretaste of the words,
he says. Noon is the page's white.
And the burden of the seeds is a mystery,
like song's scored millstone
lodged inside a bird.
A voice sleeps inside me, he promises,
and a reader will come, bringing dawn.
He throws his voice.
Now the loud sun. Now the deafening moon.
Some nights, when the whole house is asleep,
I sneak out with the pollen.

The Apple Elopes

Counting backward,
I plunge,

sprung from the branch
of a name, fast

toward the growing shade
of my ripening,

past my mother asking
from her window, *Have you seen my comb?*

asking from the porch stairs,
Who broke the clock?

Past my father warning from the edge
of the yard, *Never tithe the dark.* Oh,

they mean well, and their tones
live in what's bitter about me

and what's sweet, what's round and what's steep,
what's fragrant and what no one can marry,

me a forgetful flesh
learning the heart's tables by repetition,

me a remembering flesh weeping,
There's no going back!

A drunken flesh laughing, *There's no going back!*

My Clothes Lie Folded for the Journey

Dreamed some rain so I could sleep.

Dreamed the wind left-handed
so I could part its mane and enter
the dance that carries the living, the dead, and the unborn
in one momentum through the trillion gates.

Dreamed a man and woman
in different attitudes of meeting and parting

so I could tell the time,
the periods of the sun,
and which face my heart showed,
and which it displayed to a hidden fold.

Dreamed the world an open book of traces
anyone could read who knew the language of traces.

Dreamed the world is a book. And any page
you pause at finds you
where you breathe now,

and you can read the open
secret of who you are. As you read,

the other pages go on turning, falling
through the page before you, the sound of them the waves

. .

of the waters you walk beside
in your other dreams of the world
as story, world as song, world
you dreamed you were not dreaming.

Dreamed my father reading out loud to me,
my mother sewing beside me, singing
a counting song,

so I wouldn't be afraid to turn
from known lights toward the ancestor of light.

To Life

Who hasn't thought, "Take me with you,"
hearing the wind go by?
And finding himself left behind, resumed
his own true version of time
on earth, a seed fallen here to die
and be born a thing promised
in the one dream
every cell of him has dreamed headlong
since infancy, every common minute has served.
Born twice, he has two mothers, one who dies, and one
the mortar in which he's tried. His double
nature cleaves his eye, splits his voice.
So if you hear him say, while he sits at the bed
of one mother, "Take me home,"
listen closer. To Life,
he says, "Keep me at heart."

Seven Marys

Father John,
I have seven Marys.
What am I to do?

Ancient when I was born,
they sing to me in three colors.

Growing younger while I die faster
every year, each speaks to me
in four languages: Thinking, dreaming,
drowning, and guitar.

And one never knows what to do with her hair.
And one rocks me in and out of moonlight.
One cauterizes broken wing joints with black honey.
And one lifts my heart
onto the weighing pan opposite hunger.

Seven Marys, Father, and one
sets me on her lap and opens a book
and moves her finger from word to word

while I sound out evening's encrypted sentences.
And one is the book itself.

Seven, Father John, Marys, Father John,
the fulcrum, the eye, the heart enthroned,
the dove without person, homing.

And I can't tell the one who's always looking ahead
from the one who's always looking behind,

the one who's late for everything
from the one who's quick to remind me:

Whoever stays too long at childhood's window
leaves earth's shadow unsung.

Seven Marys, Father John, seven laughing Sarahs.

One to kiss my mouth and one to tie my hands.
One to build the pyre and one to assure me:

Don't be afraid. Find yourself
inside good-bye, one with life,
one with death.

Seven mothers, their backs turned,
walk ahead of me forever.

. .

Rachels underneath my bed, they decide
the fate of my sleep.

Bells tolling my solitude,
they are seven zeroes
trumping every count.

Marys, Father, Rachels, and Sarahs,
and I can't tell one from the other.

Is it Rachel who sings to remember the flood?
Is it Sarah who sings to forget it?
Is it Mary making my bed?
Which one can tell me
the shape of my destiny?

Descended from Dreamers

And what did I learn, a child, on the Sabbath?
A father is bound to kill his favorite son,
and to his father's cherishing,
the beloved answers *Yes*.

The rest of the week, I hid from my father,
grateful I was not prized. But how deserted
he looked, with no son who pleased him.

And what else did I learn?
That light is born of dark to usurp its ancient rank.
And when a pharaoh dreams of ears of wheat
or grazing cows, it means
he's seen the shapes of the oncoming years.

The rest of my life I wondered: Are there dreams
that help us to understand the past? Or

is any looking back a waste of time,
the whole of it a too finely woven
net of innumerable conditions,
causes, effects, countereffects, impossible
to read? Like rain on the surface of a pond.

Where's Joseph when you need him?
Did Jacob, his father, understand
the dream of the ladder? Or did his enduring
its mystery make him richer?

Why are you crying? my father asked
in my dream, in which we faced each other,
knees touching, seated in a moving train.

He had recently died,
and I was wondering if my life would ever begin.

Looking out the window,
one of us witnessed what kept vanishing,
while the other watched what continually emerged.

Parable of the Jar

By night, the jar sleeps
without dreaming, stars inside and out,
moon a few hours and sometimes
hair tied up, sometimes hair down.

By day, voices inside the jar
signal presences impossible to confirm,
despite the blinding action of the sea
and the earth's turning repose
repeated in the contours of the jar, its body
a mortal occasion of timeless law.

Questions asked into the mouth of the jar
such as: "Will I have a good death?"

Or: "Where did Noah keep the bees?
In the rafters? Were there hives
in the ribs of the boat?"

Or: "Did Jonah use soot to make the drawings
found on the inside of Leviathan's triple oven?"

Such questions
sentence the one who asks them to a life
strangely familiar, yet not
altogether one's own.

Little Ache

That sparrow on the iron railing,
not worth a farthing, purchases a realm
its shrill cries measure, trading
dying for being.

It's up to no good,
out to overturn a kingdom
just by swooping into the right kitchen,
or upsetting somebody's aim.

For my pleasure, I'll call it Good News,
or Little Egypt. For my delight,

I'll think of it as needle and thread.
Or a breathing remnant
restored to a living cloth.
Or scissors
trimming lament
to allow for everything I don't know.

For my happiness, I'll call it
Pocket Dictionary Full of Words in Another Language.

For my gladness, Feathered Interval, The Deciding Gram,
    Geronimo.

For nothing, Monument to the Nano.

Cuckoo Flower on the Witness Stand

I sang in a church choir during one war
American TV made famous.

I fled a burning archipelago in the rain,
on my mother's back, in another war
nobody televised.

In the midst of wars worldwide, many
in places whose names I can't pronounce,
my father taught me, "When asked
about your knowledge of politics, answer, 'None.' "

I doodled in the church bulletin on Sundays
while my father offered the twenty-minute Pastor's Prayer.

Every morning, I tucked Adam's promise and Jesus' disgrace
together with my pajamas under my pillow,
unable to distinguish which of them
was God's first thought, and which God's second.

When asked about my religious training, I answer,
"I seek my destiny in my origin."

Most of my life, I've answered politely
to questions put to me, speaking only when spoken to,

a sign of weakness
unbefitting of any free human being.

Therefore, for the sake of free human beings everywhere,
and because no one asked, I now say:

My voice's taper graduates to smoke,
dividing every word between us,
what was meant and what was heard.

And speech's bird
threads hunger's needle
or perishes in a thicket of words.

And so, speaking as one of the flowers,
I'll seek rest in falling.

I'll seek asylum in the final word,
an exile from the first word,
and refugee of an illegible past.

After the Pyre

It turns out, what keeps you alive
as a child at mid-century
following your parents from burning
village to cities on fire to a country at war
with itself and anyone
who looks like you,

what allows you to pass through smoke,
through armed mobs singing the merits of a new regime, tooth
    for a tooth,
liberation by purification, and global
dissemination of the love of jealous gods,
coup d'etat, coup de grace, and the cooing of mothers
and doves and screaming men
and children caught in the pyre's updraft,

what keeps you safe even among your own,
the numb, the haunted, the maimed, the barely alive,

tricks you learned to become invisible,
escapes you perfected, playing dead, playing
stupid, playing blind, deaf, weak, strong,
playing girl, playing boy, playing native, foreign,
in love, out of love, playing crazy, sane, holy, debauched,

playing scared, playing brave, happy, sad, asleep, awake,
playing interested, playing bored, playing broken,
playing "Fine, I'm just fine," it turns out,

now that you're older
at the beginning of a new century,
what kept you alive
all those years keeps you from living.

The Sea with Fish

"Years from now . . ."
"Back then . . ."
"If only . . ."
Thus, dreaming went on.

"From now on . . ."
"In that country . . ."
"Were we ever . . ."
So dreaming continued
forward and backward.

"Who would have guessed . . ."
"My father never . . ."
"My mother would always . . ."
"And then I looked up from the book and . . ."
So much for dreaming.
What about the dreamer?

Won't even answer to
On the Spot, Hidden Inside Becoming,
Stranger Going Along,
Blind but Fixed Between Wings That See.

Changing Places in the Fire

The wind in the trees
arrives all night at a word.

And the man who can't sleep
and the man who can't wake up
are the same man.

A memory of the ocean
torments the trees, a homesickness.

And the man who watches shadows of windblown leaves
and branches on the curtains,

the man who believes
a single page of the falling leaves restored
may be carried back to the living,

can't tell God's blind hand from God's seeing hand.

The wind, stranded in the branches,
like a memory of fire,

tells the oldest stories of Death
disguised as a traveler, or overlooked familiar,
friend we shunned for less
faithful playmates.

. .

And the man who's afraid of the dark
and the man who loves the dark
are the same man.

A man who's afraid to die,
he would piece the tree back together,
each part numbered and labeled:
branch, leaf, breath, cry, glance.

A man who's afraid to live,
he thinks to himself: *Postpone all morning bells.*

The ore lies awake inside the rock, a dream
of origin pealing.

The bread that rises in a house that fails,
a man weeping.

The happy grain who elects the oven,
a man laughing.

And it isn't until the wind pauses
that he thinks he knows what it says.

It isn't until the man dismantles
wind, trees, listening, does he know
there is wind, there are trees, and no listening
but a dream of listening, a dream

with infinite moving parts,
hems, pleats, train cars, recurring stairs,
an imperfect past, a rumored present,
figures multiplied inside a mirror.

It isn't until he begins to wish
to sing
the whole flower
of his breathing, does he recognize
himself, a blossom mortally wounded on its stem.

God Seeks a Destiny

The child climbs into the apple tree
and can't get down,
and can't cry out for fear
he'll wake the baby inside the house.

From where he's perched, he can see into
all of the windows at the back of the house.

There's his sister painting her eyelids
the hues of morning and evening.

There's his brother falling asleep
over his ABC's and 1,2,3's.

There's the baby
in a basket beside their mother,
whose seated at the kitchen table.
She's adding and subtracting numbers
in a dog-eared ledger.
And he can tell by her frown she's suspicious
Death owns the figures,
and the decimal is a double agent.

And where is his father?
In the room with the shut curtains, of course.
He's talking to God again, who plays
hide and seek among His names.

. .

But wasn't it God who lured the child
ever higher into the tree with glimpses
of God's own ripening body?

Stranded thus in a branching net
staked between earth and sky, between
present summer and future summer,
isn't the boy God's prey?

And who wakes now but God in the boy's flesh
and astonished bright blood,

as his hands suddenly see,
his feet begin to find
his weight alive,
his mind aligned
not with the fate of a stunned will

but some greener knowing and
feeling his way back to earth.

God's destiny is safe
for now inside the child.

Secret Life

Alone with time, he waits for his parents to wake,
a boy growing old at the dining room table,

pressing into the pages of one of his father's big books
the flowers he picked all morning

in his mother's garden, magnolia, hibiscus,
azalea, peony, pear, tulip, iris;

reading in another book their names he knows,
and then the names from their secret lives;

lives alchemical, nautical, genital;
names unpronounceable fascicles of italic script;

secrets botanical
description could never trace:

accessory to empire, party to delusions of an afterlife,
kin to the toothed, mouthed, furred,

horned, brained. Flowers
seem to a boy, who doesn't know better, like the winged,

the walking, the swimming, and crawling things abstracted
from time, and stilled by inward gazing.

Copying their pictures, replete with diagrams, he finds
in the words for their parts,

. .

the accounts of their histories,
and their scattered pollen,

something to do with his own fate
and the perfection of all dying things.

And when it's time, he discovers in the kitchen
the note left for him that says

his parents have gone and will return by noon.
And when it's time, the dove

calls from its hiding place
and leaves the morning greener

and the one who hears the dove more alone.

The Lives of a Voice

1. Dear and With

The boy didn't want to let go of the bird.
As long as he closed it
between both hands, several worlds—

not just inside and out,
not just fear and desire,
not just dream and appetite, claws,
hands, and wild eyes—several worlds
remained one, inviolate.

Until the moment the thing set free
flew beyond recovery.

And the bird became various birds,
the one became many

indefinite parts: wings
and the shadows of wings,
cries and the color of his mother's hair,
fate and a lifetime of longing.

2. A Voice's Gaze

Wait, wait, wait, what are you saying?
The wind is principle? The dove is potential?

The dove unseen, but heard
by the one who is hidden

below the eave his own hearing makes?
What are you saying?

Our listening is principle?
Our speaking is potential?

Do you mean our hearing makes a house
for our singing?

Are you saying our singing
indicates the bounds of our feeling,
lays open the laws of our being?

What do you mean a voice walks barefoot
among the names of things?

    . .

What do you mean,
pulled from the fire, a voice thrives,
undisguised in open season?
Whose voice? What fire? Wait,
wait, wait, what are you saying?

3. Tethered

The dove outside my window sounds hurt
all the time.

No country of origin.
Living in occupied territory

all the time. In the shadow
of an unattainable heaven,

burdened by a memory
of perfect orchards trimmed by unseen hands.

Maybe being winged means being wounded
by infinity, blessed by the ordeal
of freedom. At crossroads

all the time, all the time rocking
chair, rocking horse, rocking train, rocking boat,

a heart born to a station of oars,
an office of wings, born flying, born

falling between heads and tails,
trespass and grace, home and wilderness.

. .

Could be thinking is curved, like the earth,
and feels, therefore, heavy.

Could be wings are an affliction,
a different kind of tyranny,
and flying is no better than walking upright.

4. My Joy

Winter must be almost over,
the mourning dove is back.

I heard it this morning
as I stepped out of my bath.

I couldn't find it, though,
in any window.

Maybe it will venture to show
when trees start to ache and green.

It didn't say a word
about where it wintered,

whether on some rocky cliff face, with sun
and wind ministering to it

(sun saying *veritas,* and *vir unus,*
wind saying *enath,* and *athanasias,* and *spiritus*

rector), or whether at some resort
in Florida. I don't know

     . .

if it's the same dove as last year,
the dove returned, the word restored,

or is this a new bird,
a new page pressed by winter's hand,

a new song creased under winter's iron.

5. Fire Enthroned

Not another word about the dove.
Or the child, or the shadow
of the mother's voice, or the dove's voice,
or the child without a voice, or the mother's shadow,
a garment drying on the hedges

beside the river,
where the child hides, where the dove lives,
where death walks with no one watching.

Not another word about the mother's voice,
a boundless house and acre the child, spoken for, ranges,
the child without a voice, the child unspoken.

Not another word about the dove's changing pitch,
now a narrow doorway to the sea,
now an unheated room in autumn,
now a sodden bed of leaves.

The dove beside the water
builds its fine nest, does its fine math
with sticks and string and time,

. .

confiding to the light there
what it heard
about the pollen, the nettles, the mother.

No more children's games, counting
the dove's calls and the child's cries,
keeping score for hunger and plenty.

A dove's peeled breast could barely feed a soul.
The hunger it tolls is the child's
whole inheritance.

Not another word about death,
or how the dove's tremors
are only the lapsed echoes
of that first voice, the fire enthroned,
the fire alive inside each thing
woven of dust and yearning.

Not another word about the child who,
suddenly remembering his death,
tells his mother, "By then
I'll know what to call
the color of your eyes."

The Shortcut Home

In my sister's story,
God can't find us
in any of His coat pockets,
not in the empty, and not in the filled.
We're in none of His hands, the kind or the terrible;
none of His shoes, the giant or the minute.
And neither are we hiding inside the apples,
neither in the perfect nor the ruined.
Not in the first mouthful, and not in the last.

In my brother's story,
our death sings to us from the highest branch
of the oldest tree the birds remember
in song, and we wander our father's house
in search of the origin of the hours.

In my story . . . But I don't have a story.
All I have are a few names of the flowers:
Morning Glory, Seven O'clock, Mother of Wings,
Story Carried Backward Up a Stairs. All I have
is a sown path I follow back to sleep:
Painted Face, Clouded Pane, Song in a Jar,
Burning Threshold, Bloody Scrimmage,
Voice Strewn on the Rocks.

Standard Checklist for Amateur Mystics

A lamp, so you can read the words on the tablet.
A hand to copy the sentences you find.
A hand for you to rest your head.

Feet to dance the gist of what you find.
A bird to scour your heart.
A bird to help you pronounce the sentences.

Breath to fan the fire's nest.
A kiln to test the choice.
A crown to keep underfoot.

Two eyes to see the one in one.
Three to see the two in one.
Seven to see the all in one.
A hand to cross out your name.

A donkey to carry your shit.
A monkey to filch change and food.
A brother to point the way.
A sister to redeem the refused.
A sister to ransom the straw.
A sister to wake you with kisses
when you've fallen asleep at your opus.

Bring Home Her Name

Whose house is this? Nobody knows.
Birds flying in and out of every window
all year long and doors swinging wide
in the wind both ways, toward the glow

of an imagined past, and toward the bride,
that fleeing girl, the future. She hides
by changing, escapes by standing still.
The secret of possession? Go outside.

She'll come to rest inside you. Leave your will.
Meet your dark lender, Evening, below the hill.
Her father, he'll tell you her name.
Then you'll ransom the hours and heart you spent
playing house on property lent,
taste her name and for what your life is meant.

A Winter Day

Snow on the roof.

All afternoon I read in the sunlit room
and jotted down words now and then,
troubled now and then by thoughts
of how long
the light would last. Now

shadows have amassed
at the feet of objects, and soon
the unmade bed, the scattered papers, the books
in rows and piles, the cups of tea gone cold,
the plates and crumbs from the lunch we shared,

will all look stranded in the rising dark,
like wreckage from a ship spoiled by storm.
Until I turn on a lamp
and see

the heart's sphere squared to make a room,
the mind's love entrusted
to a few words on a page.

Virtues of the Boring Husband

Whenever I talk, my wife falls asleep.
So, now, when she can't sleep, I talk.
It's like magic.

Say she hasn't had a good night's sleep in a week,
feels exhausted, and lies down early
in the evening,
but begins to toss and turn.

I just lie down beside her,
prop my head up in one hand and say,
"You know, I've been thinking."

Immediately she calms down,
finds a fetal posture,
and tucks her head under my arm.

I know she lies dispersed, though in one body,
claimed by rabble cares and the need to sleep.

"Will you stay?" she asks.

"I'm right here," I answer.

"Now, what were you saying?" she wonders,
and so I talk.

. .

"It isn't that lovers always meet in a garden,"

and already her eyes
get that dizzy look, like she can't focus.

"Go ahead," I tell her, "close your eyes."

"OK," she says, "but keep talking." And so I do.

"It isn't that lovers always speak
together in a house by the sea, or in a room
with shadows of leaves and branches
on the walls and ceiling.

It's that such spaces emerge
out of the listening
their speaking to each other engenders.
I mean, maybe . . ."

And she sighs. Her breathing begins to slow.
And I remember something I heard somewhere:

Every so many breaths, a sigh.
Every so many sighs, sleep.

Or was it: *Every so many sighs, death?*

I go on talking, now stroking her head,
pushing her hair back from her forehead,

clearing her bright brow,
and listening for her next sigh.

"Maybe the face-to-face true lovers enact
manifests a prior coincidence
of heaven and earth, say, or body and soul,
equal opposites exchanging
and combining properties in perpetual transformation:

shore and not shore, sea and sky,
room and a world, the gazer and the gazed upon."

Little twitches run the length of her, beginning
with her arms, then her legs, then her feet, as though
tensions were being fired from her body.

She mumbles the beginning of a word.
I go on talking.

"Maybe the union of lovers is an instance
of a primary simultaneity, timeless,
from which arises the various shapes of Time and duration:
arrival, departure, waiting, resuming,
fountain, terrace, path, an eave.

. .

And maybe any world is born, is offspring,
of the liaison between
God and Mind,
Mind and Mind's source."

I count her second sigh, lower, longer.

"Or maybe God says *I love you!* and the whole
universe, consciousness included, is a shape
of that pronouncement.

Or maybe there's no *You* in that,
but only *I love!* ringing,
engendering all of space, every quadrant
an expression of God's first nature: *I love!*

Or maybe a *You*
arises as echo, the counter-ringing,
to the sovereign *I love!*

and we're the *You* to the Source's *I,*
the second person to God's first personhood.

Then, to surrender any sense of an *I*
is to feel our true condition, a *You*
before God, and to be seen.

        . .

Being seen: the crowning experience
and mystery of a *You.*

Maybe, too often, we mistake
the guest for the host,

confusing the *I* and the *You.* And yet, maybe
out of that confusion more worlds arise."

By now, she's barely listening, if at all.
I lower my voice and go on rambling,
afraid she'll wake if I stop too soon.

"Maybe love for God amounts
to the Beloved returning
the Lover's gaze.

And out of that look and looking back,
all of our notions
of space, home, distance,
beginning, end, recurrence,
death, debt, fruition, number, weight
emerge; all are issue

of that meeting between
lover and lover, our souls' intercourse
with what it loves."

       . .

By now her jaw has gone slack, her fingers loose
where earlier they were clenching the edge of the blanket,
and I'm almost whispering.

"Maybe it's true, what sages have said,
I don't know if I'm remembering it right.
Something about moving up a ladder of love.
Maybe we learn

to love a person, say, first as object,
and then as presence, and then as essence,
and then as disclosure of the divine,

or maybe all at the same time,
or discovering over time
each deeper aspect to be true.

And maybe our seeing it in another
proves that face inside ourselves.

Oh, I don't know. You sleep now."

And then I stop talking, kiss her forehead,
and wait a minute
before leaving the bed and closing
the door behind me.

To Hold

So we're dust. In the meantime, my wife and I
make the bed. Holding opposite edges of the sheet,
we raise it, billowing, then pull it tight,
measuring by eye as it falls into alignment
between us. We tug, fold, tuck. And if I'm lucky,
she'll remember a recent dream and tell me.

One day we'll lie down and not get up.
One day, all we guard will be surrendered.

Until then, we'll go on learning to recognize
what we love, and what it takes
to tend what isn't for our having.
So often, fear has led me
to abandon what I know I must relinquish
in time. But for the moment,
I'll listen to her dream,
and she to mine, our mutual hearing calling
more and more detail into the light
of a joint and fragile keeping.

Living with Her

1.

She aches.
And would have me think
it had to do with rivers.

She talks.
Her voice a wheel
and every station on it.

And what she doesn't say
makes the sound of wind in the trees.

She walks,
her path the years sown behind her.

She sleeps.
And her sleep becomes
the river I build
my house beside.

So, on which bank of the river
am I now, waking or dreaming?

She says, *Come away from the window. Lie down.*
There's no dark out there that isn't first in you.

· ·

Close the door. Come lie down.
There's no ocean out there not already in you.

What a narrow residence,
the lifetime of her eyes.

2.

She opens her eyes
and I see.

She counts the birds and I hear
the names of the months and days.

A girl, one of her names
is Change. And my childhood
lasted all of an evening.

Called *Light*, she breathes, my living share
of every moment emerging.

Called *Life*, she is a pomegranate
pecked clean by birds to entirely
become a part of their flying.

Do you love me? she asks.
I love you,

she answers, and the world keeps beginning.

Dying Stupid

My name is written in heaven and so is yours.
Heaven above is heaven below.
But what do I know?

It's possible I never lived
and might die stupid, never knowing
if being born is good or bad.
And is death worse or better than what?
And is each person's death the same?
How can that be if every life is different?
Is every life different?

"All being tends toward fire," says the fire.
"All being tends toward water," says water.
"Light," says the light.
"Wings," say the birds.
"Voice," says the voiceless.

And to the mysteries of appearance add Song.
And to the mysteries of disappearance
add world-creating, world-destroying Time.
But what do I mean by "world"?
Worlds? Each a world? Worlds within a world?
What do I mean when I say, "The world
and I are imperfect friends?"

· ·

What do I mean when I say, "The voices of children
shepherding noon signals thunder
and springtime at large among the glyphs?"

Have I clung too long to notions I arrived at
playing alone as a boy;
sentences my father said to copy
a hundred times each night into a notebook?
What can I say I know for sure?

Days grow old, but Day? Never.
Nights are broken by days, a thread skipping,
but Night? Never.

And in the shadow of our human dream of falling,
human voices are Creation's most recent flowers,
mere buds of fire
nodding on their stalks.

Station

Your attention please.
Train number 9, The Northern Zephyr,
destined for River's End, is now boarding.

All ticketed passengers,
please proceed to the gate marked *Evening*.

Your attention please. Train number 7,
Leaves Blown By, bound for The Color of Thinking

and Renovated Time, is now departing.
All ticketed passengers may board
behind my eyes.

Your attention please. Train number 4, The Twentieth Century,
has joined The Wind Undisguised
to become The Written Word.

Those who never heard their names
may inquire at the uneven margin of this story
or else consult the ivy
lying awake under our open window.

Your attention please,
The Music,
arriving out of hidden ground

and endlessly beginning, is now the flower,
now the fruit, now our cup and cheer

under branches more ancient
than our grandmother's hair.

Passengers with memories of the sea
may board leisurely at any unmarked gate.

Fateful members of the foam may proceed to cloud and
        Veronica.

Your attention please.
Under falling petals, never think about home.

Seeing begins in the dark.

Listening stills us.

Yesterday has gone ahead
to meet you.

Your attention please. Train number 66,
Unbidden Song, soon to be
the full heart's quiet, takes no passengers.

. .

Please leave your baggage with the attendant
at the window marked: *Your Name Sprung from Hiding.*

An intrepid perfume is waging our rescue.

You may board at either end of Childhood.

Acknowledgments

GRATEFUL ACKNOWLEDGMENT is made to the editors of the following publications, where some of the poems first appeared: *Lyric, Poetry, Orion, The Pushcart Prize XXXII: Best of the Small Presses, Runes, Speakeasy, Spirituality and Health,* and *World Literature Today.*

Very special thanks to the following people, whose faith and encouragement made this book possible: Jill Bialosky, Diane Bilyiak, Robert Bly, Eavan Boland, Alison Granucci, Gerald Stern; to Greg Garrett and Christopher Greene at Truself Studios for recording the CD; and to Donna Lee, for listening to the poems over and over, and for teaching me to make the bed.